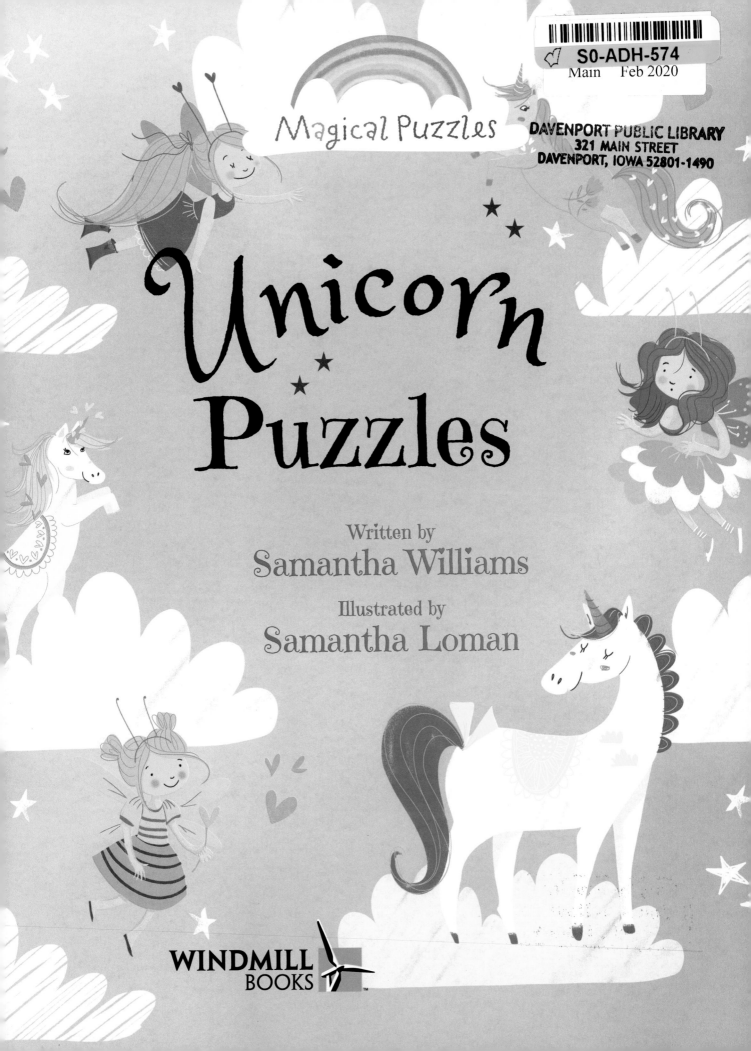

Magical Puzzles

Unicorn Puzzles

Written by
Samantha Williams

Illustrated by
Samantha Loman

WINDMILL
BOOKS

Published in 2020 by **Windmill Books**, an imprint of Rosen Publishing
29 East 21st Street, New York, NY 10010

Illustrated by Samantha Loman
Written by Samantha Williams
Edited by Susannah Bailey
Designed by Well Nice Ltd

Cataloging-in-Publication Data

Names: Williams, Samantha. | Loman, Sam.
Title: Unicorn puzzles / Samantha Williams, illustrated by Sam Loman.
Description: New York : Windmill Books, 2020. | Series: Magical puzzles
Identifiers: ISBN 9781538391846 (pbk.) | ISBN 9781538391860 (library bound)
| ISBN 9781538391853 (6 pack)
Subjects: LCSH: Picture puzzles--Juvenile literature. | Unicorns--Juvenile literature.
Classification: LCC GV1507.P47 W55 2020 | DDC 793.73--dc23

Manufactured in the United States of America

CPSIA Compliance Information: Batch #BS19WM:
For Further Information contact Rosen Publishing, New York, New York at 1-800-237-9932

Contents

Twin Teaser

These unicorns are frolicking in the magical meadow.
But can you tell which two are twins?

Find Me!

The baby unicorns are playing hide-and-seek! Can you spot all seven of them?

5

Party Prep

Springblossom loves getting dressed up!
Which of these silhouettes is an exact match for her?

#selfie

These unicorn friends have been taking photos, but one looks slightly different. Can you figure out which one?

Which Way?

Can you help Blossom find the path
back to the pink palace?

Finish

Start

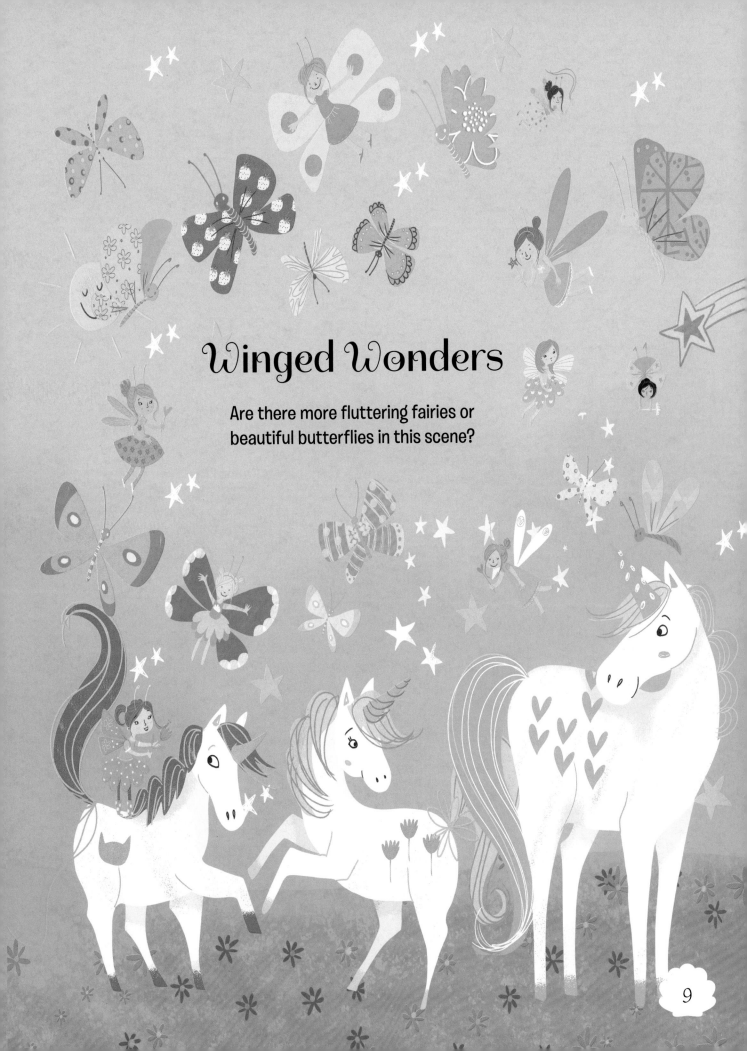

Winged Wonders

Are there more fluttering fairies or beautiful butterflies in this scene?

Beautiful Bows

Which unicorn is wearing each pretty patterned bow?
Follow their twisting tails to find out!

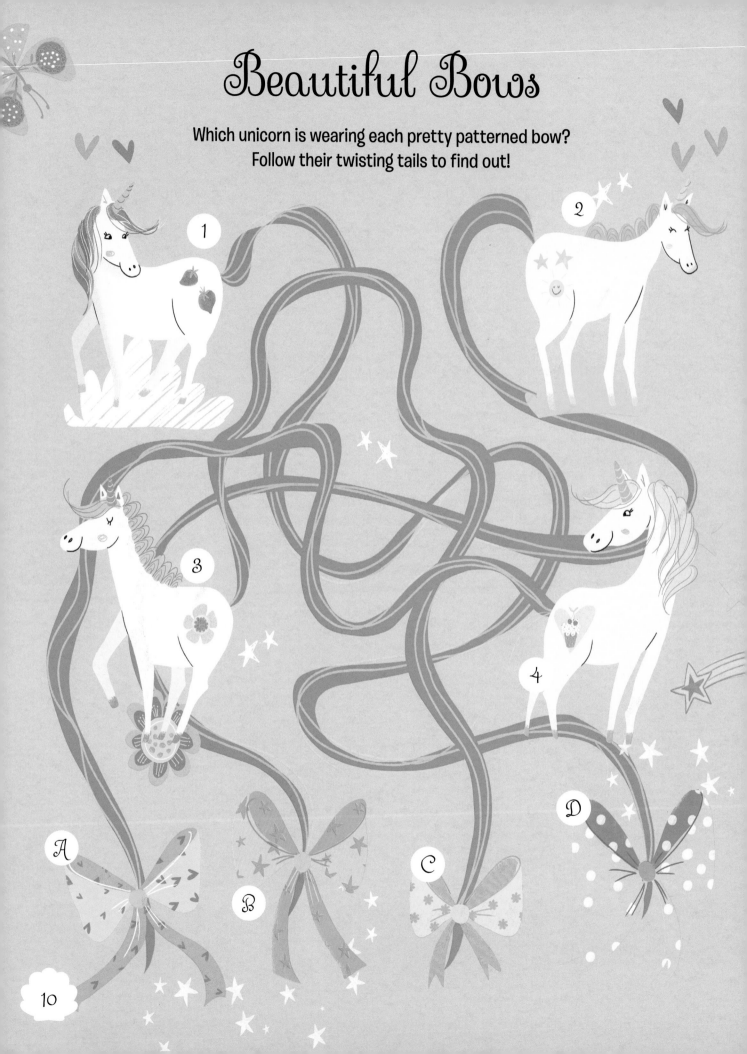

1

2

3

4

A

B

C

D

Knock! Knock!

It's getting dark, and Gumdrop can't remember the secret password to let her into the castle. Can you unscramble the letters so she can get inside?

AFIYR

WIPSHRES

Lost Jewels

The Unicorn Queen has lost her beautiful necklace! Can you help her find it? She needs to search her stones in a particular order, going up, down, right, and left, but not diagonally.

1

2

3

Start

12

Finish

Magical Memories

Look at this picture for two minutes.
Then turn the page and answer the questions
without looking back.

Magical Memories

Write your answers on a separate
piece of paper.

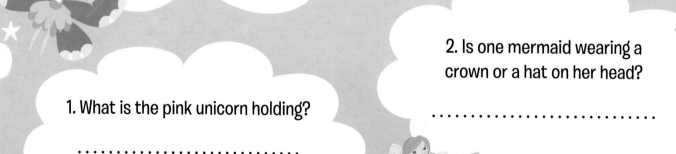

2. Is one mermaid wearing a
crown or a hat on her head?

. . . .

1. What is the pink unicorn holding?

. . . .

3. How many fairies are there?

. . . .

4. How many unicorns have
bows on their tails?

. . . .

5. How many mermaids
are there?

. . . .

6. What is sitting on top
of the toadstool?

. . . .

Magical Unicorn Name

Your birth month + your fave baby animal = your unicorn name! For example, if you were born in April and like kittens, your name would be Golden Starlight. Write down yours on your notebook!

JANUARY	SPARKLY	JULY	SHINY
FEBRUARY	DIAMOND	AUGUST	RAINBOW
MARCH	CRYSTAL	SEPTEMBER	DREAMY
APRIL	GOLDEN	OCTOBER	TWIRLY
MAY	GLITTERY	NOVEMBER	CANDY
JUNE	TWINKLY	DECEMBER	SHIMMERY

PUPPY	SUNSHINE
KITTEN	STARLIGHT
DUCKLING	SUNFLOWER
LAMB	BUTTERCUP
PIGLET	PRINCESS
BUNNY	MOONBEAM
CHICK	FIRE GLOW

My unicorn name is:

....

My friend's unicorn name is:

....

15

Perfect Presents

It's Rainbow's birthday! Can you unscramble the letters to figure out what all the other unicorns have bought her?

1 CIEOOKS

2 ERPFUEM

3 SRDSE

4 LOTHCES

5 UPKACCSE

Pet Puzzle

The unicorns have been exercising their pets, but their leashes have become tangled. Can you find out which pet belongs to which unicorn?

Party Perfect

These unicorns have dressed for a party in exactly the same outfits,
but one of them isn't dressed quite the same as the others.
Can you find who it is?

Cute Kites

These unicorns are flying kites, but their strings are all in a tangle. Can you figure out which kite belongs to which?

Rainbow Land

Can you put the pieces of this magical scene back together?
Which piece doesn't belong at all?

In the Clouds

Loveheart needs to find a way across the cloud kingdom to join the fairies. Can you help her cross, following the order here?

Start

Finish

Pretty Patterns

Draw your own unicorns on a separate piece of paper. Now decorate the horns, heads, and necks of your unicorns with swirls and stars!

Magical Feast

The unicorns are having a magical meal!
Can you figure out what they're serving for each course?

Starter
SKLRAPE IEP

....

Main course
CHCOATLOE
BREINWOS

....

....

Dessert
WELTREMOAN
ELIHGDT

....

....

Deck the Halls!

The unicorns and fairies are decorating the Christmas tree. Can you find eight differences between these two festive scenes?

24

Castle Games

The unicorns have hidden themselves all over the magical castle. Can you find all 10 of them?

Leaping High

Which unicorn is the best at rainbow jumping?
Calculate who has the highest score to find out!

1/2 of 28

1

2

30 - 15

3 x 6

3

4

36 ÷ 4

Magical Unicorns

Which unicorn is wearing a bow that matches the color of their horn?

Pretty Ribbons

Violet can't find her special bow. Can you help her?
It's the only one that doesn't have an exact match,
and she's not already wearing it.

Flashing Fireflies

The unicorns are watching the pretty fireflies in the sky. Can you tell which one looks a little bit different?

Answers

Page 4: Twin Teaser

Page 5: Find Me!

Page 6: Party Prep

Page 7: #selfie

Page 8: Which Way?

Page 9: Winged Wonders
Butterflies: Twelve, Fairies: Nine.
There are more butterflies.

Page 10: Beautiful Bows
1 D
2 B
3 C
4 A

Page 11: Knock! Knock!
The secret password is:
Fairy Whispers.

Page 12: Lost Jewels

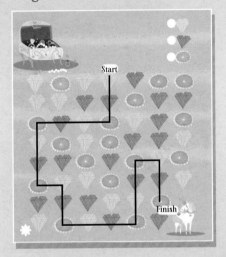

Page 18: Party Perfect

Page 21: In the Clouds

Page 13: Magical Memories

1 A balloon.
2 She's wearing a hat.
3 There are four fairies.
4 Two unicorns.
5 Four mermaids.
6 A snail.

Page 16: Perfect Presents

1 Cookies
2 Perfume
3 Dress
4 Clothes
5 Cupcakes

Page 17: Pet Puzzle

1 D
2 C
3 A
4 B

Page 19: Cute Kites

1 C
2 D
3 A
4 B

Page 20: Rainbow Land

Piece A does not belong.

Page 23: Magical Feast

Starter: Sparkle pie
Main course: Chocolate brownies
Dessert: Watermelon delight

Page 24: Deck the Halls!

Page 25: Castle Games

Page 27: Magical Unicorns

Page 29: Flashing Fireflies

Page 26: Leaping High

Number 3 is the best at rainbow jumping.

14

15

18

9

Page 28: Pretty Ribbons